BEJEWELLED TREASURES

The Al Thani Collection

Arts Décoratifs; and Claire Martin at the Petit Palais, Musée des Beaux-Arts de la Ville de Paris. I also thank Vivienne Becker for sharing her expertise on the rings formerly owned by Maharaja of Indore.

In Mumbai, Viren Bhagat and his sons Jay and Varun took Joanna Whalley and me to their workshops in early 2015; in Jaipur, Rajesh Ajmera and Rajiv Arora arranged for us to visit a number of precious stone dealers and polishers in the city, and to spend time with Manish Sain and the craftsmen of the Amrapali workshops. All of this was both fascinating and illuminating. It demonstrated beyond doubt, as did the new pieces in traditional style in Santi Choudhary's Royal Gems & Arts showroom in Jaipur, that contemporary skills in Indian jewellery can be of the highest order.

Prakriti Ranjan Goswami, Himani Pande, Gunjan Verma and Kanika Gupta kindly arranged for me to see the Lala Deen Dayal archive at the Indira Gandhi National Centre for the Arts in Delhi, and for key images to be included in this book.

In Paris, it was a great pleasure to meet Joel Arthur Rosenthal and Pierre Jeannet, and to see some of JAR's current jewellery collection.

In addition, I am indebted to all the following who have provided factual information, advice, reference sources, images or other help: Naman Ahuja; Alice Bailey; Usha Bala Krishnan; Laura Barber; Kara Bargmann; René Brus; Francesca Cartier Brickell; Christopher Cavey; Beatriz Chadour-Sampson; Steven Cohen; Derek Content; Debra Diamond; Max Donnelly; Ann Eatwell; Mel Evans; John Falconer; Zahra Faridhany Akhavan; Katherine Field; Margot Finn; Maya Foo; Arun Garg; Sophie Gordon; Tom Grosvenor; Christine Guth; Michael Hing; Karin Hofmeester; Roselyne Hurel; Peter Jarman; Priya Kapoor; Jack Kemp; Sandra Kemp; Betsy Kohut; Saskia Konniger; Pramod Kumar KG; Vikash Lall; Vishnu Lall; Gaby Laws; Leela Meinertas; Leslee Katrina Michelsen; Jagdish Mittal; John Moghtader-Mojdehi; Elise Morero; Choodamani Nandagopal; Jack Ogden; Keelan Overton; Anamika Pathak; Clare Phillips; Marcia Pointon; Malini Roy; Patricia Schwaiger; Robert Skelton; Donna Stevens; Dawn Sueoka; Giles Tillotson; Živa Vesel; Ming Wilson; Laor Zak; Benjamin Zucker.

Not least, I thank my husband, Souren Melikian, for his advice and constant support, as well as several crucial translations of passages in Persian texts.

Introduction

The jewellery, jewelled objects, jade and unmounted precious stones in this book have been selected for the Victoria and Albert Museum's exhibition *Bejewelled Treasures: The Al Thani Collection*. Together, they illustrate court arts of the Indian subcontinent and demonstrate the influence of Europe on traditional Indian ornaments, as well as the much more significant influence of India on European jewellery. The exhibition also includes three exceptional pieces generously lent by Her Majesty the Queen: two historic spinels (the precious stone that was more highly prized than any other at the Mughal court in the seventeenth century) and the jewelled gold bird that once perched on the canopy over the throne of the famous South Indian ruler Tipu Sultan.

This book begins with an essay on the theme of bejewelled splendour in India, followed by a catalogue of the objects that reflects the structure of the exhibition. The broad chronological range, covering the early seventeenth century to the present day, makes the Al Thani Collection unique in its field.

Many of the pieces in *Bejewelled Treasures* were published in the 2013 book *Beyond Extravagance*. It was edited by Amin Jaffer, International Director of Asian Art at Christie's and curator of the Al Thani Collection, and written by Vivienne Becker, Jack Ogden, Katherine Prior, Judy Rudoe, Robert Skelton, Michael Spink and Stephen Vernoit. Sixty-five objects were shown in *Treasures from India: Jewels from the Al-Thani Collection* at the Metropolitan Museum, New York, in 2014, accompanied by a book written by the show's curators Navina Najat Haidar and Courtney Ann Stewart. The larger and different selection for the V&A includes some important early pieces acquired since the publication of *Beyond Extravagance* (a forthcoming new edition by the same authors will include all later acquisitions). To avoid duplication, full bibliographies are given here only for these new objects; for the rest, bibliographic information and extensive technical descriptions may be found in the catalogue entries of *Beyond Extravagance*. As would be expected in such a challenging field as traditional Indian jewellery, in which reliable information concerning provenance is crucial to establish authenticity but extremely rare to find, the dates assigned to individual objects sometimes differ between *Beyond Extravagance*, *Treasures from India* and this book. Given this, the presence in the Al Thani Collection of a small number of fully documented objects of the seventeenth and eighteenth centuries is highly important.

Fig. 3 The Mughal emperor Farrukhsiyar (r.1713–19) bestows a jewel
Opaque watercolour and gold on paper
Mughal, c.1713–19
The David Collection, Inv. no. 26/1982

The art historian Vidya Dehejia draws attention to the information about early jewellery in South India provided by temple inscriptions. She notes that nearly 100 record in extraordinary detail the donations of gold vessels, jewellery and other artefacts made to temple treasuries by the Chola royal family. In the early eleventh century, for instance, the emperor Rajaraja's sister, Kundavai, made a single donation of 15 ornaments for the bronze statues of deities in the Sri Rajarajeshvara temple. These included a crown weighing the equivalent of over 1,844 grams (4 lb), set with precisely 859 diamonds, 309 rubies and 669 pearls.[32] Contemporary sculpture provides an indication of what these jewels and vessels looked like; the temple treasures that survive and feature in publications are of considerably later date (fig. 9).[33]

In all these temple inscriptions the excellence of many of the stones in the jewelled artefacts is described. It is striking, however, that so too are the multiple imperfections of numerous others, even though the technical treatises advise that flawed stones should be avoided. While the pre-eminence of diamonds, rubies and pearls seems to confirm the relative values of precious stones given in Sanskrit texts, emeralds and sapphires are notably absent. In the case of emeralds this may indicate a lack of availability: until the sixteenth century, the major sources were Egypt and Habachtal (Austria), though recent research suggests that the Swat Valley in present-day Pakistan may have supplied emeralds much earlier than the apparent discovery of deposits there in the eighteenth century.[34] Sapphires are traditionally supposed to be worn with caution by many non-Muslims in the Indian subcontinent because of their perceived potential to exert a malign influence, and their omission from the temple donations may reflect this.[35]

Fig. 8 The Maharaja of Rewah (r.1880–1918)
Photograph
c.1880–90
The British Library, Photo 209 (17)
The maharaja wears *navaratna* armlets.

Fig. 9 'Jewels used in the temple
Great Temple, Madura, Madras'
1880s
V&A: National Art Library, 46.D.54

عمل بالچند

Fig. 10 Shah Jahan and his sons on a globe
Balchand
Opaque watercolour and gold on paper
Mughal, c.1628–30
Chester Beatty Library, In 07A.10

INNOVATION AT THE MUGHAL COURT

In the sixteenth century, the global trade in precious stones expanded radically at the same time as a major new power with a profoundly different culture arrived in the subcontinent.

The Mughal empire, founded in 1526 by Babur, the Central Asian leader of an invading army and descended from the conqueror Timur, had a fragile beginning. However, by the end of the century, the emperor Akbar (r.1556–1605) had established Mughal rule over all the central and upper regions of the subcontinent, including present-day Pakistan, Bangladesh, Kashmir and much of Afghanistan. In the process of his aggressive military expansion, the Mughal armies seized the treasuries of Hindu rulers in Rajasthan and Muslim sultans in Gujarat and Bengal. Tribute including precious stones and jewelled artefacts added to the empire's wealth that was passed on to, and augmented by, Akbar's successors in the first half of the seventeenth century (figs 10 and 12).

In the same period, a small European settlement founded in 1510 became the capital of the Portuguese State of India (Estado Português da Índia). Goa, on the west coast, was a major commercial centre at the heart of the well-established Portuguese colonial empire that stretched from North Africa to the Japanese coast, and Portuguese ships dominated the Indian Ocean. Goa was also a very significant trading centre for precious stones in the East for most of the sixteenth and seventeenth centuries, based on its relative proximity to a number of gem sources, including Sri Lanka, Burma and the Deccan.[36]

In Goa's shops on its famous Rua Direita, diamonds, rubies, sapphires, spinels, pearls and many other semi-precious stones could be bought. An early sixteenth-century Portuguese poem about Goa lists all these, and also mentions 'emeralds of princely value', almost certainly referring to the spectacular stones of Colombia.[37] Spanish galleons brought these from the newly exploited South American mines to Seville, where Portuguese merchants could buy them to trade in Goa. From there, the emeralds of considerable size and deep colour found a ready market in the courts of the subcontinent.

The greatest demand for precious stones came from the Mughal court. One of the reasons Akbar sent his embassies to Goa was to buy them. In 1601 he wrote to the Portuguese Viceroy, Aires de Saldanha, to request that credit be extended to the imperial ambassador for the purchase of gemstones and other items worthy of his treasury.[38] Jewel merchants travelled from Goa to the great Mughal cities in order to gain direct access to the vast purchasing power of the royal family and its circle. The success of Portuguese gem traders is reflected in the journal of Sir Thomas Roe, the English ambassador to the court of Jahangir, in 1616. He recorded that the merchants came annually from Goa with rare things to sell to the emperor, and 'rich presents' from the Viceroy. One particularly delicate negotiation with the emperor over trading rights for the English was abruptly interrupted when the Portuguese entered, carrying 'divers rubies, ballaces [i.e. spinels], emrallds, and jewells sett to sell; which so much contented the King and his great men that we were for a tyme eclipsed'.[39]

Akbar had so many unmounted precious stones that by the 1590s one of his 12 treasuries was reserved exclusively for them, with another for jewelled artefacts. The description of this treasury for precious stones in the official history of his reign, written in Persian and completed by 1596, demonstrates that there was

2 **Necklace**

Spinels on a necklace of cultured pearls
with a dyed green beryl bead
L 53 cm

The impressive size of the spinels suggests they came from royal treasuries in the Indian subcontinent. All have Mughal titles engraved on them. Moving clockwise from upper right these read:[1]

- 79.50 carats, inscription to Jahangir partly removed by polishing: *Jahangir sha[h-e] A[bar shah]* = King Jahangir [son of] King Akbar

- 111.46 carats, inscribed (probably in recent times) to 'Alamgir: *'A[lamgir] shah ibn-e Shah-e Jahan 1071*, King 'Alamgir son of Shah Jahan AH 1071/AD 1660–1

- 132.73 carats, inscribed to Jahangir and partly polished away: *Jahangir shah-e Akbar shah 1017* (= AD 1608–9)

- 144.58 carats, inscribed to Jahangir and Shah Jahan: *Jahangir shah-e Akbar shah 107 saheb qeran-e sani 1037*, Second Lord of the Conjunction AH 1037/AD 1627–8

- 82.82 carats, inscribed to Jahangir, Shah Jahan and 'Alamgir: *Jahangir shah-e Akbar shah 1016* (AD 1607–8) *saheb qeran-e sani 1043, 6*, Second Lord of the Conjunction 1043 [regnal year] 6 = 8 July 1633 – 26 June 1634 *'Alamgir shahi 1070*, 1, [belonging to] King *'Alamgir 1070* [regnal year] 1 = AD 1659

- 61.50 carats, inscribed to Jahangir, with another inscription partly polished away: *Jahangir shah-e Akbar shah la'l-e ?j … li*. If this reads *la'l-e jalali*, as the residual letters suggest, it links the stone directly to Akbar. In the 1590s, the emperor's chronicler named the best seal engravers attached to the court. One, Maulana Ibrahim, was an Iranian from Yazd whose specialist task was to engrave the words *la'l-e jalali*, or 'glorious spinel', on all the most valuable of these stones.[2] This simultaneously alluded to the emperor's title, Jalal ad-Din Muhammad Akbar.

- Pendant: 202.67 carats, inscribed to 'Alamgir and Ahmad Shah, who established the Durrani dynasty in Afghanistan: *'Alamgir shah bin Shah Jahan*, 'Alamgir, son of Shah Jahan *Ahmad shah durr-e durran* 1168, Ahmad Shah, 'Pearl of Pearls' AH 1168/AD 1754–5

1. The weights of each spinel are those given by Christie's in 2014; some of the details in the readings and transliterations given in the catalogue are modified here, and corrections made to errors in the date conversions. It should be added that the inscriptions include a few that do not seem to be authentic, and others, notably those that have been partly removed by polishing, that have been filled with lac. This makes it impossible to establish whether engraving tools or other means produced them.
2. Blochmann and Phillott 1977, vol. 1, p. 55 (with *la'l* mistranslated as 'ruby').

Published: Christie's, Geneva: *Magnificent Jewels*, 14 May 2014, lot 177.

3 The Nabha spinel

Spinel engraved with imperial Mughal inscriptions, with silk threads and seed pearls, and a gold pin

L 4.6 cm W 2.4 cm

123 carats

The Royal Collection/HM Queen Elizabeth II, RCIN 11526

In 1901, Sir Hira Singh, the Sikh Raja of Nabha (r.1877–1911), was unable to attend the forthcoming coronation of Edward VII in London. Instead, he sent this spinel engraved with the titles of three Mughal emperors: Jahangir, dated AH 1017/AD 1608–9 (detail below); Shah Jahan, dated AH 1038, regnal year 1/AD 1628–9; and 'Alamgir, dated 1070, regnal year 1/AD 1659–60. The fact that the inscriptions of Shah Jahan and his son were both added in their coronation years may have enhanced its appeal as a gift for Edward VII's coronation. This loyal supporter of the British wrote to the new king that the stone was 'a badge of the Moghul Empire which is now under His Majesty's sway', and could therefore 'properly belong to the Emperor of India'.

Published: Stronge 1996, p. 10; Stronge (ed.) 1999, p. 238, cat. 205, illus. p. 29.

4 Seal ring with spinel inscribed to Shah Jahan

Spinel dated 1643, set in a modern Indian enamelled gold ring

H 2.7 cm W 2.1 cm

The inscription in reverse has been partly worn away by polishing, but its fine engraving is still clearly legible. It gives Shah Jahan's title, Second Lord of the Conjunction (*sahib qeran-i sani*), the Islamic era year 1053, and the regnal year 12, dating it to between 22 March and 16 August 1643.[1] The hemispherical stone is ribbed, which reflects the light internally and enhances the colours.

1. Begley and Desai (eds) 1990, p. xxxvii for a table of Shah Jahan's regnal years.

8 The 'Agra diamond'

Cut-cornered, rectangular mixed-cut, fancy intense pink diamond
H 1.8 cm W 1.7 cm
28.2 carats

The delicate colour combined with considerable size make this diamond extremely unusual. Like the 'Idol's Eye', facts mingle with flights of wild fantasy in the many accounts of its history. Balfour writes that it was owned by the first Mughal emperor Babur after his invasion of Hindustan in 1526, remained in the imperial treasury until Nadir Shah's raid on Delhi in 1739, and then somehow returned to India. Here, the story continues, English officers who had seized it from the imperial treasury in Delhi during the uprising of 1857 planned to conceal it in fodder so that it could be smuggled on board a ship bound for England inside the horse that ate it.[1]

The first verifiable reference to the 'Agra diamond' appears in the 1860 catalogue of the jewels owned by the Duke of Brunswick, which states that he had bought it in 1844 from 'Blogg'. George Blogg, a partner in the London firm of diamond merchants Blogg and Martin, may well have supplied the spurious history and been the originator of the myth that the stone was seized by Babur in Agra. This diamond has also been recut over time, reducing its weight considerably from 41 carats in 1844.

1. Balfour 2000, p. 28.

Published: *Catalogue de brillants et autres pierres précieuses de son Altesse Monseigneur le Duc souverain de Brunswick-Luxembourg...* (Paris, 1860); Christie's, London: *The Agra Diamond and two other important coloured diamonds*, 20 June 1990, pp. 13–27; Khalidi 1999, pp. 68–9; Balfour 2000, pp. 28–33; Ogden in Haidar and Sardar 2015, p. 327.

Fig. 23 The Mughal courtier Rustam Khan (d.1658)
Hunhar
Opaque watercolour and gold on paper
Mughal, c.1650
Chester Beatty Library, In 07B.35
Before defecting to the court of Shah Jahan, Rustam Khan was in service to one of the sultans of the Deccan, where he may have acquired the splendid cut diamond set into the pommel of the dagger, which can be seen beneath his left hand.

9 The 'Pink Golconda diamond'

Brilliant-cut, oval-shaped, internally flawless type IIa
H 1.84 cm W 1.38 cm D 0.5 cm
10.46 carats

The striking characteristics of this diamond are its delicate pink hue and flawless limpidity. When it was sold at auction (then mounted in a platinum ring set with small diamonds), the Gübelin laboratory report supplied a carefully worded description: 'diamonds of this type, exhibiting an antique cutting style as well as a superior quality, are very rare and will most certainly evoke references to the historic term of Golconda'. Lack of precise information about its history, as with many diamonds, means that with such stones 'seldom can an Indian origin be proved', as Jack Ogden notes.[1] Mines outside the subcontinent have also produced pink diamonds.

1. *Beyond Extravagance* 2013, p. 381.

Published: Sotheby's, New York: Magnificent Jewels, 9 December 2010, lot 467; *Beyond Extravagance* 2013, p. 381, cat. 127.

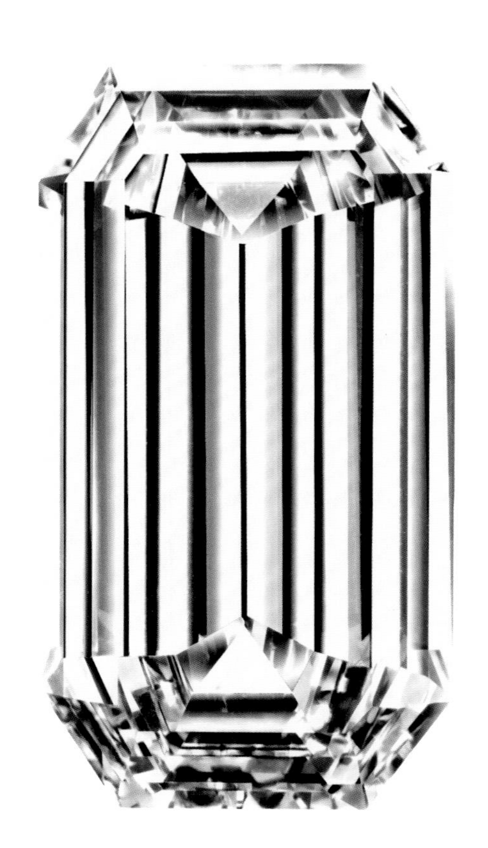

10 The 'Mirror of Paradise'

Step-cut, octagonal, grade D, internally flawless type IIa
H 3.46 cm W 1.85 cm D 0.86 cm
52.58 carats

This octagonal step-cut diamond is graded 'type IIa' and internally flawless, with the highest 'D colour' grade, meaning that it is actually completely colourless and is therefore of the greatest degree of purity. These exceptional qualities are traditionally associated with some of the finest Golconda diamonds, but are not exclusive to them. Unknown before its certification by gemmological laboratories in 2000, the diamond had acquired the name 'Mirror of Paradise' when it was first exhibited in Rome in 2002.[1]

1. I am grateful to Amin Jaffer for supplying data on the diamond.

Published: Bari, Cardona and Parodi 2002, p. 80, fig. 17; Christie's, New York: *Magnificent Jewels*, 10 December 2013, lot 496.

11 Diamond pendant

Cut-cornered rectangular portrait cut, grade J, type IIa
H 2.57 cm W 3.31 cm D 0.18 cm
20.22 carats

12 **Necklace**

Emeralds and pearls on silk thread

The very large size of the 32 emeralds, some of which are ribbed, and of the 59 natural pearls, suggests they originally belonged to a royal treasury. They would have been worn in necklaces as emblems of sovereignty in the Mughal empire. Portraits of Hindu rulers of Rajasthan in the eighteenth and nineteenth centuries (fig. 24) indicate a marked preference for emerald, or emerald and pearl necklaces.

Fig. 24 **Maharaja Pratap Singh, aged 29 (r.1778–1803)**
Sahib Ram
Opaque watercolour and gold on cloth
Jaipur, 1793
Maharaja Sawai Man Singh II Museum, City Palace, Jaipur

The Court

Many of the emblems of royalty used within the Indian subcontinent have an ancient lineage. In the seventh century, the Buddhist monk Xuanzang mentions that the emperor Harsha and the King of Assam accompanied an image of the Buddha in procession, holding a parasol and fly whisk above the image respectively.[1] Fly whisks indicated divinity and are depicted in early Hindu and Jain sculpture held by attendants next to the deity. The fly whisk and parasol were simultaneously the essential attributes of Hindu kings,[2] and served the same purpose in the Muslim courts of the subcontinent as they did in later courts, regardless of the religion of the ruler. Royal ownership of swords and daggers might also be indicated by parasols inlaid in gold on the blades (cat. 24).

The other key emblem of sovereignty is the throne, which was usually of gold, often heavily bejewelled and sometimes with a gold canopy. Jewellery, from necklaces with multiple strings to turban ornaments and thumb rings, also proclaimed royal status. In the period when Mughal power was at its height, these were worn only by the ruler, usually a man, and his family. As central power declined, this prerogative became less strictly observed.

Luxury artefacts were an integral part of courtly life, whether in formal ceremonies or in the private lives of the elite. The presentation of *pān*, the edible leaf wrapped around chopped areca nuts, spices and lime, subtly hinted that a formal audience had come to an end, but was also enjoyed in private entertainments. In courtly settings, these leaf pouches were kept in covered boxes made of jewelled or enamelled metal or jade (cats 31 and 32). Within the Mughal empire, tobacco was also added to the mixture after it was brought back to the court in 1604 by the emperor Akbar's emissary to the Deccan, where it had been introduced by the Portuguese.[3]

With the arrival of tobacco, the habit of smoking through a water pipe (*huqqa*) gradually took hold (cat. 34). Jahangir's hostility meant that it never became part of Mughal court life during his reign, and depictions of smoking are rare in paintings of court scenes under his immediate successors. By the eighteenth century, paintings of the ruler smoking a huqqa are commonplace throughout the subcontinent, from the Hindu hill kingdoms of the Panjab to the sultanates of the Deccan. The exception is the Sikh courts of the Panjab, where most of the attributes of royalty formulated by the Mughal emperors were adopted, but religious prohibition ruled out smoking. Many globular or bell-shaped huqqa bases in metal, hardstone and glass, and mouthpieces usually of jade or agate that fit onto the 'snake' connecting smoker and huqqa base, have survived.

1. Ali 2004, p. 117.
2. Gonda 1969, p. 37.
3. Subrahmanyam 1990, p. 55, for the Portuguese and tobacco; Qaisar 1982, pp. 119–23, for smoking at the Mughal court.

Fig. 29 **The Mughal emperors Akbar, Jahangir and Shah Jahan enthroned**
Bichitr
Opaque watercolour and gold on paper
Mughal, c.1630–1
Chester Beatty Library, In 07A.19

23 **Wine cup of the Mughal emperor Jahangir**

Mottled grey nephrite jade
Mughal, dated AH 1016, regnal year 2/AD 1607–8
H 5.7 cm W 5.4 cm
Formerly in the Guennol Collection

This is the earliest dated jade artefact that can be linked directly and without doubt to any Mughal emperor. Its simple form is ornamented with very fine calligraphy in three registers. A royal dedication in monumental *sols* script occupies the central band. It announces that the cup was made for Jahangir and was completed in AH 1016/AD 1607–8 (opposite, above). The inscription on the upper border in *Nasta'aliq* script (opposite, below) states that it was the personal wine cup of the emperor and made in his second regnal year, therefore between 28 April 1607 and March 1608. An object of such importance would very likely have been presented to the emperor during the New Year (*Nowruz*) celebrations, when the elite of the empire exchanged presents of great opulence and rarity, poets composed special verses, and artists and craftsmen revealed their new work.

The Persian verses ornamenting the cup include a quatrain composed by a much earlier poet, with a second quatrain written in the manner of early Persian poetry. A.S. Melikian-Chirvani plausibly suggests that the author of the seventeenth-century verses was the craftsman who actually made the cup. Sa'ida-ye Gilani, the superintendent of the royal goldsmiths under Jahangir and Shah Jahan, was also a great master of engraving calligraphy on hardstones. In addition, he was a poet rewarded by Jahangir for his skill in producing verses containing chronograms, in which the numerical value of the letters in a particular phrase add up to the year in which the poem was composed. The identification of Sa'ida as the maker of the cup is further strengthened by the script, which is closely related to the hand of the engraver of an inscription on a spinel owned by Jahangir, known to have been written by this imperial goldsmith.[1] Cups of similar shape can be seen in contemporary paintings and drawings.

1. Melikian-Chirvani 2001, p. 98.

Published: The cup has often been published since its appearance at auction (Sotheby's, London: *Medieval, Renaissance and Later Works of Art*, 16 December 1971, lot 70). The inscriptions were first published in *The Guennol Collection*, vol. 2, pp. 62–5 (Rubin (ed.) 1982). The most complete bibliography is in Melikian-Chirvani 2002, p. 133, note 26. This author also provides photographs of the calligraphic decoration, reproduces the inscriptions and gives a corrected English translation with analysis of the Persian verses. Subsequently, the cup has been reproduced in Stronge 2011–12, fig. 1.

42 **Dagger**

Nephrite jade hilt and scabbard chape with rubies and emeralds in kundan settings; watered steel blade
The hilt, Mughal, eighteenth century, with later pommel and modern blade
L 39.5 cm

Contemporary sources in the reign of 'Alamgir (1658–1707) make frequent reference to the presentation of daggers with jade hilts to favoured individuals, reflecting the greater availability of the raw material. Paintings of Mughal emperors in the first half of the eighteenth century often depict them with jewelled jade-hilted daggers tucked into their sashes (see fig. 3). The forms of dagger pommel vary considerably. The most elaborate incorporate floral elements, but this model is unusual. The jade also differs from that on the lower section of the hilt and the setting of the stones is by a different hand, all suggesting this is of relatively recent manufacture.

Published: *Beyond Extravagance* 2013, p. 101, cat. 29.

43 Crutch handle

Nephrite jade with floral decoration in low relief and with rubies, emeralds and diamonds in kundan settings
Mughal, eighteenth century, the stones on the top added later
H 4.6 cm W 12 cm

Published: *Beyond Extravagance* 2013, p. 105, cat. 38.

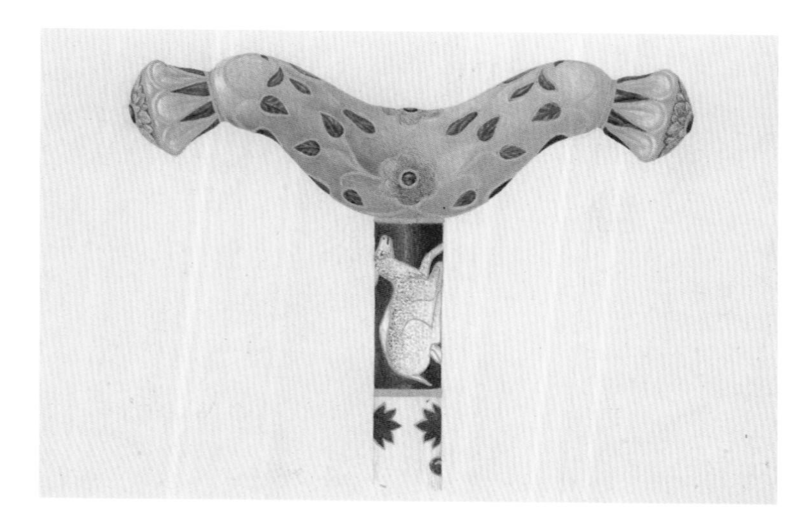

Fig. 41 Crutch handle
Opaque watercolour on paper
Jaipur, c.1890
V&A: IS.29-1992
Given by Mrs G.M. Hendley

Fig. 42 Four ascetics
Opaque watercolour and gold on paper
Mughal, eighteenth century
V&A: IS. 219-1952

44 **Thumb ring**

Nephrite jade with rubies, emeralds and diamonds in kundan settings
Mughal, c.1700–30
L 5 cm W 3.5 cm D 2 cm

From the reign of Jahangir, thumb rings worn as emblems of royalty began to be made in jade from Khotan. Paintings also depict them, possibly of jade or agate, suspended on silk threads attached to the sashes of the emperor and his sons (p. 88). In the reign of ʿAlamgir, hardstone thumb rings seem to have fallen out of favour with the emperor himself, but later paintings demonstrate that the fashion was revived under his successors. The profile of this ring is more slender than datable rings of the mid-seventeenth century, and the pale jade has a slightly greenish hue associated with later periods.

Published: *Beyond Extravagance* 2013, p. 186, cat. 50.

45 **Thumb ring**

Nephrite jade with rubies and emeralds in gold settings
Mughal, c.1700
H 1.6 cm W 2.9 cm D 3.9 cm
Formerly in the Guennol Collection

Although the gemstones are not of the superlative quality of those in thumb rings of the seventeenth century, this was probably made in a court workshop. In the eighteenth century, although the empire was gradually disintegrating, craftsmen continued to produce jewellery and artefacts for the emperors. These are depicted in portraits, that demonstrate they were now also worn by high-ranking individuals outside the royal family.

Published: *The Guennol Collection* vol. 2, pp. 71–3 (Rubin (ed.) 1982); Bala Krishnan 1999, p. 223.

46 **Turban ornament**

Gold with diamonds in kundan settings,
enamelled on the back
Jaipur, late nineteenth century
H 10.5 cm W 19.2 cm

The briolette diamond drops on this piece, enamelled in the typical style of Jaipur, are seen on several jewels from the collection of the Nizams of Hyderabad.[1] They reflect European fashions of the early twentieth century. Similar diamond drops ornament the large turban jewel worn by Asaf Jah VII, Osman 'Ali Khan, in the 1906 wedding portrait taken by the court photographer, the renowned Lala Deen Dayal.[2]

1. See Bala Krishnan 2001, pp. 82, 94, 107, 157.
2. Illustrated in *Beyond Extravagance* 2013, p. 235.

Published: *Treasures from India* 2014, pp. 64–5.

67 **Pair of earrings**

Gold set with emeralds, rubies and with later pendant pearls and red glass terminals
Probably Hyderabad, c.1900
H 3.9 and 3.8 cm W 4.3 cm

These earrings are in the classic form called *chandbali*, or crescent moon. The setting of the stones, and the form of the cross posts that would run through the pierced ear, compare with the same features on a pair of diamond and emerald gold *chandbali* earrings in the V&A, made for the donor's mother in Hyderabad in about 1900.[1]

1. IS.25–2008.

Published: *Beyond Extravagance* 2013, p. 274, cat. 99: 'Provenance: by repute, nizams of Hyderabad'.

68 **Pair of earrings**

Silver set with diamonds, and with later pendants of pearls, enamelled gold and green glass
Probably Hyderabad, c.1900
H 4.6 cm W 5.1 and 4.8 cm

The form is characteristic of Hyderabad. The Indian journalist Renuka Narayanan, recalling visits in recent times, describes wandering through jewellery shops, where she bought 'those graceful "moon hoops" for the ear, typical of the city, called *chandbali*'.[1]

1. Imam (ed.) 2008, p. 281.

Published: *Beyond Extravagance* 2013, p. 274, cat. 100.

75 **Turban ornament**

Diamonds and a large sapphire in platinum
India c.1920, modified c.1925–35
H 7.4 cm W 6 cm
Sapphire 109.5 carats

The pins on the back of this jewel suggest that it was originally designed as a brooch or pendant, with the palmette pointing downwards. A later clip and the addition of five diamonds on long curving terminals change the orientation and give it the appearance of a turban aigrette.[1] It reputedly belonged to Ranjitsinhji, Jam Saheb of Nawanagar. His great friend Jacques Cartier, writing about 'The Nawanagar Jewels' after the maharaja's death, noted that Ranjitsinhji had decided after his accession to make the State Collection of jewels 'second to none in India'.[2] He collected rubies, pearls, diamonds and, especially, emeralds, with passion and knowledge, and in 1931 commissioned a necklace described by Cartier expert Hans Nadelhoffer as 'the most precious cascade of coloured diamonds known to history'.[3] Sapphires are not mentioned in Cartier's essay, and nothing seems to be known of how the ruler may have acquired this piece.

1. Prior in *Beyond Extravagance* 2013, p. 276.
2. Wild 1934, pp. 323–6.
3. Nadelhoffer 2007, p. 322.

Published: *Beyond Extravagance* 2013, p. 276, cat. 104; *Treasures from India* 2014, p. 91.

76 **Turban aigrette of the Maharaja of Nawanagar**

White gold set with diamonds, in two detachable parts with a diamond-set pendant
India, c.1935
H 15 cm W 7 cm D 2.5 cm

The 17 largest diamonds (excluding the pendant) together weigh 152.64 carats. They were originally set in a turban aigrette made for the Maharaja of Nawanagar, Ranjitsinhji, presumably when he became ruler of this western Indian princely state in 1907. Photographs demonstrate that Ranjitsinhji habitually changed the appearance of the aigrette by attaching different rosettes to the upper section.[1] Ranjitsinhji's nephew, Digvijaysinhji Ranjitsinhji, succeeded him as maharaja in 1933, and had the aigrette redesigned. A bolder effect was created by its more compressed form and by adding another sizeable diamond. The aigrette is unmarked, but was probably made by a leading Indian jeweller in Bombay or Delhi. The firm of Gazdar, for example, founded in Bombay in 1933, supplied a number of princely houses including Nawanagar.

1. Prior in *Beyond Extravagance* 2013, p. 275.

Published: Christie's, Geneva: Jewels, the Geneva Sale, 17 November 2010, lot 292; *Beyond Extravagance* 2013, p. 275, cat. 103; *Treasures from India* 2014, pp. 92–3.

Fig. 58 **Ranjitsinhji, Maharaja Jam Sahib of Nawanagar (r.1906–33)**
Photograph
c.1910
Yves Cywie Private Collection

TWO ELEMENTS FROM A CARTIER ENSEMBLE OF EMERALD JEWELLERY

77 Clip brooch

Carved emerald in platinum mount by Cartier, 2010
H 5.3 cm W 4.05 cm
141.13 carats

Published: *Beyond Extravagance* 2013, pp. 95–6, cat. 14; *Treasures from India* 2014, pp. 106–7; *Cartier: Style and History* 2013, p. 164, cat. 215.

78 Clip brooch

Emeralds and diamonds in platinum,
with black enamel
Cartier, Paris, 1925, modified in 1927
H 6.7 cm W 4.4 cm
Hexagonal emerald c.88.03 carats; central cabochon emerald c.15.65 carats

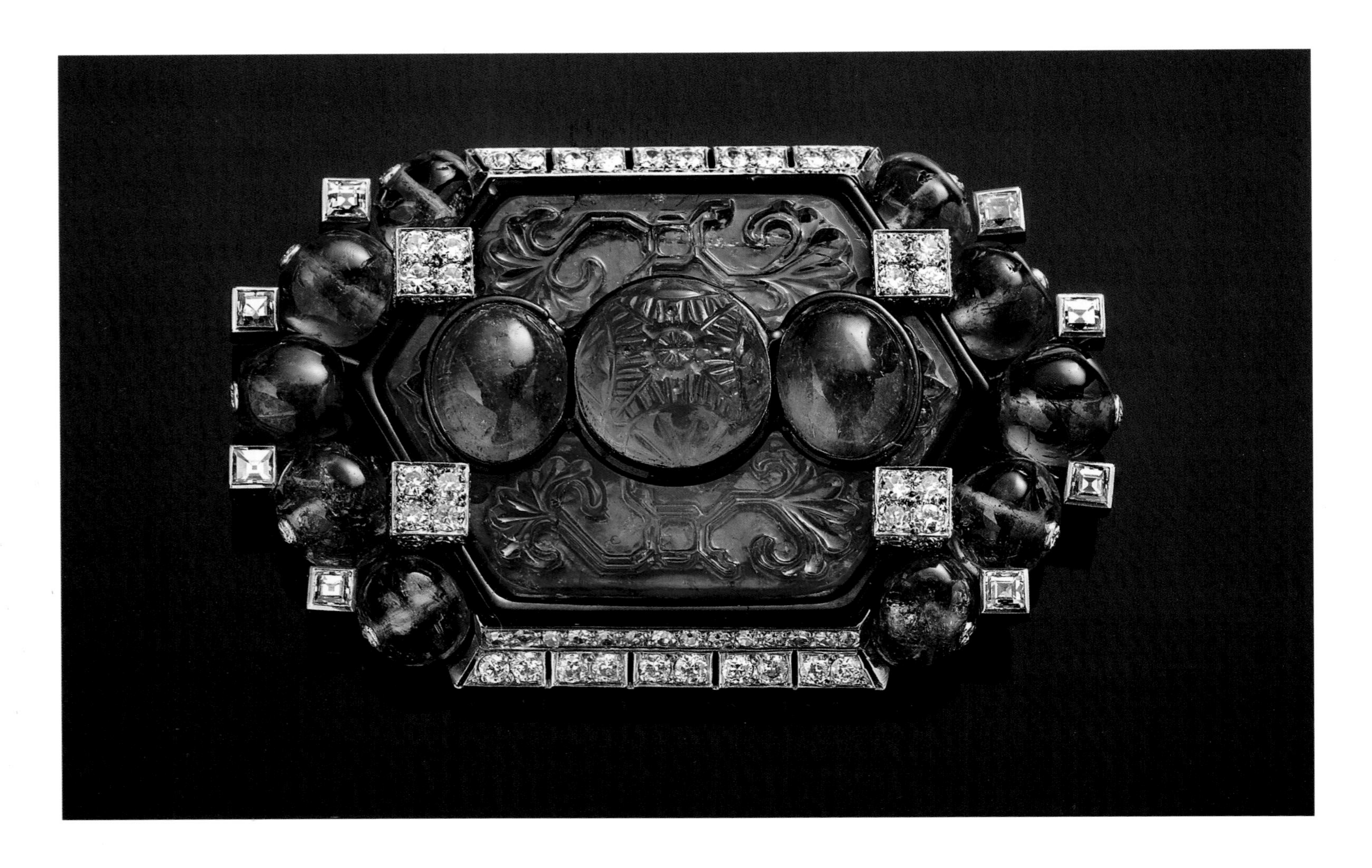

79 **Belt brooch**

Emeralds, sapphires and diamonds
in platinum and gold
Cartier, Paris, 1922
H 4.2 cm W 8.5 cm
Octagonal emerald approximately 38.71 carats

Cartier's belt brooches were in vogue for a short period in the early 1920s and this piece was made for stock in 1922.[1] Its form, and the combination of blue and green stones, both derive from the fascination with Iran and Mughal India that permeated the arts of the period. The outline of the palmettes on either side of the central rectangular element, emphasized by a delicate border of calibré-cut sapphires, combines Chinese and Middle Eastern influences. This is characteristic of the eclectic use of sources of artistic inspiration at Cartier, particularly in the 20-year period beginning in 1910 when the designer Charles Jacqueau worked closely with Louis Cartier.[2] The resulting pieces moved away from the precisely observed detail of paintings and objects to a more whimsical evocation of 'the Orient'.

1. Rudoe in *Beyond Extravagance* 2013, p. 319.
2. Nadelhoffer 2007, p. 135.

Published: *Beyond Extravagance* 2013, pp. 319–10, cat. 110; *Treasures from India* 2014, p. 103; *Cartier: Style and History* 2013, p. 153, cat. 192.

80 **Shoulder brooch**

Platinum and gold, set with emeralds,
diamonds and rubies, with black enamel
Cartier, London, 1924; the tassel was re-created from
original records by Cartier workshops, Paris, 2012
H c.15 cm; brooch H 3.3 cm W 7 cm

Two emeralds carved on both sides in India, in similar style but of slightly different size and each with diamonds in kundan settings, were incorporated into this piece made at a time when Cartier was firmly established in India. As Judy Rudoe points out,[1] the form of the brooch mimics that of the traditional Indian *bazuband*, the hinged jewel worn on the upper arm. The carved emerald terminals may even have originally belonged to a *bazuband*.

1. Rudoe in *Beyond Extravagance* 2013, p. 320.

Published: *Beyond Extravagance* 2013, p. 320, cat. 111; *Treasures from India* 2014, pp. 104–5; *Cartier: Style and History* 2013, p. 153, cat. 193.

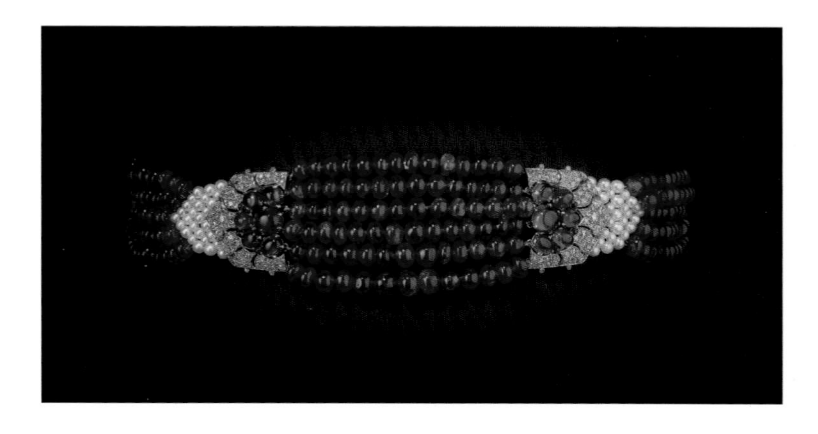

Fig. 63 **Maharani of Patiala**
Vandyk
Photograph
London, 1931
Majithia – Shergill Collection

81 **Choker**

Rubies, diamonds and pearls in platinum
Restored and restrung by Cartier Tradition, Geneva, in 2012 to the original design created by Cartier, Paris, in 1931 for the Maharaja of Patiala
H 2.2 cm L 33.3 cm

In 1925, when the Maharaja of Patiala asked Cartier, Paris, to remodel pieces from his treasury, it was the biggest commission the firm had ever had from a single client. The maharaja continued to patronize Cartier and other jewellers in Paris in the 1930s. In 1931 he bought an ensemble of three necklaces of rubies, pearls and diamonds for one of his wives (above, right). The smallest element, a choker, then disappeared from public view. Research undertaken by Cartier's archivists discovered that a bracelet sold at auction in 2000 incorporated diamond-set elements from the 1931 choker and some of its rubies. The firm acquired it in a subsequent auction. Antique rubies were added, allowing the lost Patiala choker to be re-created from the original design, using the original terminals.

Published: *Beyond Extravagance* 2013, p. 322, cat. 114; *Treasures from India* 2014, pp. 108–9; *Cartier: Style and History* 2013, p. 300, cat. 437.

82 **Brooch or hat jewel**

Rubies and diamonds in platinum with a white gold pin
Marked 'PT 950' on the reverse and 'Or' on the pin
France (?), c.1935
H 6.9 cm W 4.2 cm

The unusual shape of this brooch suggests that it was inspired by Indian turban jewels and may have been worn in a hat.[1] It is probably French, given the 'Or' mark on the white gold pin, but cannot be attributed to a specific firm. Although the 1930s were characterized by a taste for 'white jewellery' where diamonds were set in platinum or white gold, the continuing engagement with India of leading jewellers meant that polychromatic jewellery was still fashionable.

1. Rudoe in *Beyond Extravagance* 2013, p. 323.

Published: *Beyond Extravagance* 2013, p. 323, cat. 115; *Treasures from India* 2014, p. 111.

95 **The 'Star of Golconda' brooch**

opposite

Diamonds in platinum and white gold with a large pendant diamond
Cartier, Paris, 2011
Pendant diamond L 3.81 cm W 2.41 cm D 0.72 cm
57.31 carats: mixed-cut, pear-shaped, grade H, internally flawless

The name given by Cartier to the 57.31-carat diamond forming the pendant of this brooch romantically associates it with the legendary Indian mines.[1] The simplicity of the design of the specially commissioned piece recalls those made by Cartier, New York, for historic stones in the early twentieth century.[2]

1. GIA report 17449518.
2. Nadelhoffer 2007, pp. 320–2.

Published: *Beyond Extravagance* 2013, p. 381, cat. 126 (diamond only).

96 **Ring**

Emerald and pearls with gold
JAR, Paris, 2013
H 2.5 cm W 3 cm

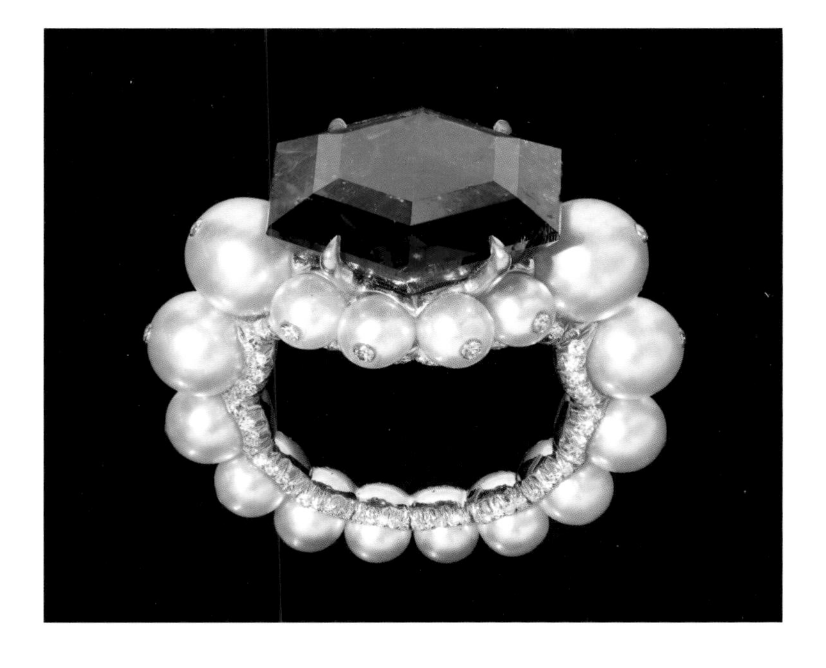

The deep saturated green of the emerald exemplifies Joel Rosenthal's love of colour and of stones with remarkable individuality. The open back setting allows the faceting to be seen through the limpid clarity of the emerald held by four delicate gold claws. The pearls, carefully chosen to diminish regularly in size across the outer surface of the hoop, are each set with a minute diamond in gold. Clusters of diamonds frame the gold cups in which the pearls rest. The combination of emeralds and pearls is relatively rare in jewellery by JAR, but was used in a ring made in 1988.[1]

1. *JAR Paris* 2002, cat. 320.

98 Ring

Engraved Mughal emerald in gold set with two diamonds
Bulgari, Rome, c.1980
Marks: BVLGARI 950. H 2.4 cm W 2.8 cm D 2.1 cm
Emerald W 1.9 cm D 1.8 cm

The curved back of the emerald is covered with irregular facets in three registers, suggesting it was cut within the Mughal empire. The flat front is engraved with a Persian quatrain that is an invocation to God:

> O Beloved One and Lord, by the truth of existence
> Six bounties increase that which you sent
> Knowledge, action and generosity,
> Faith, security and health.[1]

A date beneath the verse is engraved in minute scale and is slightly damaged. It appears to be the year 1011 of the Islamic era (21 June 1602 to 10 June 1603).

1. I am indebted to A.S. Melikian-Chirvani for his translation.

97 Necklace

Diamonds, white metal and an emerald bead
The diamond beads antique probably assembled in recent times in India
L 35 cm maximum

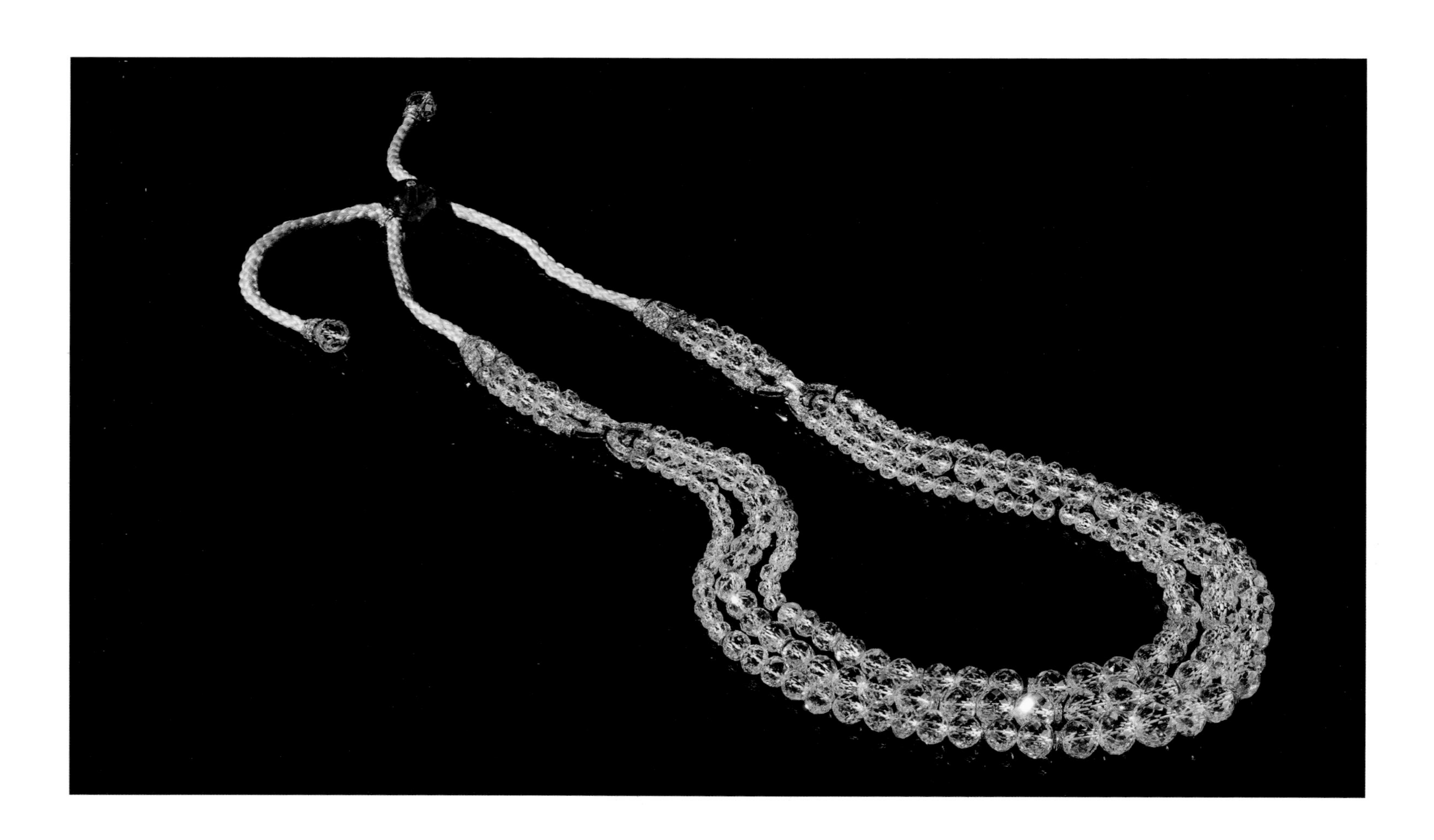